Also by Gus Speth

*Red Sky at Morning: America and the Crisis of the
Global Environment*

*The Bridge at the Edge of the World: Capitalism, the
Environment, and Crossing from Crisis to Sustainability*

*America the Possible: Manifesto for a New Economy*

*Angels by the River: A Memoir*

*What We Have Instead: Poems*

# It's Already Tomorrow

Poems by
## Gus Speth

# It's Already Tomorrow

Poems by
Gus Speth

## SHIRES ❦ PRESS

4869 Main Street
P.O. Box 2200
Manchester Center, VT 05255
www.northshire.com

It's Already Tomorrow
Poems
©2020 Gus Speth

ISBN: 978-1-60571-497-4

Design/production, Anne Pace
Cover art by the author

Printed in the United States
2020

This book is available from
Northshire Bookstore at www.northshire.com,
Amazon.com, barnesandnoble.com, Ingram,
and indie bookstores across the country at IndieBound.org

Northshire Bookstore is a family-owned, independent bookstore in
Manchester Ctr., VT and Saratoga Springs, NY

*For Cameron, Rodgers, Lilla,*
*Charlotte, Grace, and James*

# — Contents —

## Love

## Howl

# — *Contents* —

## Laugh

## Remember

*After the final no there comes a yes.*
*And on that yes the future world depends.*

—Wallace Stevens

# Love

## An Error in Time and Space

You are gone tonight, and the vacant space
beside me is a vastness into which I reach.

I feel only absence and longing,
cold sheets in a wintry November.

There is a not rightness about it,
an error in time and space.

I remember two weeks ago dining
out across the river with easy friends.

While waiting for the food to arrive,
we went around the table answering—

what is the secret of a long marriage,
since we had all been long married.

Spurred by the moment, I answered
devotion, loyalty, forgiveness.

I should have remembered the words
stitched on the pillow in your chair:

Happiness is being married to your best friend.
I long for my friend this night.

## Lift Up These Eyes

We chased away the mist,
opened up the day,
blew holes in the clouds,
and called down the sun.
It lit the wet rocks where
we dropped to our knees,
leaned over the edge, followed
the red talus slope down and down
as it fell to green embroidery
framing the dark river below.

The breeze began to stir.
We heard the tent door flap.
Little Cas is crawling out
into the morning light. She lifts
her head, sees us, and sends
an ear-to-ear crescent-eyed grin—
a moment of shared delight
as bright as the new-found sun.
Good morning, Cas, we say
in all the languages we know.

## For a Moment

A porcelain white and windy day
a day to watch the chickadees

A foot or more of light new snow
building drifts along the road

The scattered birdfeeders
pecked down now and empty

She makes her way across the yard
her white cap glowing in the sun
a dusty yellow encircles her neck
a scarf the Magnolia Warblers wear
and on her slender back a royal blue
the color of the Indigo Buntings

She lifts herself arms reaching up
up to dislodge a pair of frozen feeders
For a moment I can imagine
her taking off in graceful flight

## Generations

I plodded downstairs early this morning
and was sipping a much-needed coffee
when I noticed the yard had more than its
normal complement of robins to see.
These early birds are getting worms, I thought,
worms the heavy rain last night has brought.

I saw something very strange in the yard,
and at that moment our son phoned us.
Char's a busy guy, driving then to work.
There's always family news to discuss.
It's a short drive and is his main time free.
Still, he shares this time with his mom and me.

I listened, but the robins were distracting.
Three were close together, each bird dancing
a quick two-step, moving across the yard.
The largest robin led this prancing
followed closely by two smaller ones—
their triangle hopped around in the sun.

Their movement seemed quite random, but then
the lead bird spotted something by the tree.
She paused while the two trailing birds jumped
quickly to the front, and then there were three
beaks all pecking at the unlucky worm.
My guess this is bird parenting confirmed.

Our son said his daughters have a busy day,
both a soccer game and a hip-hop class.
He'll cover one and his wife the other.
The bird triangle hopped on to new grass.
I thought then how these events well captured
the artistry of lives being nurtured.

## Bach Hears Music

What does Bach think when he hears Klemperer
conducting his great Mass in B Minor?
Well, he shouts to a bright heaven, Hallelujah!
And when he hears Aretha Franklin and Paul Simon,
Harry Nilsson, Miles Davis, The Beatles,
Loretta Lynn, Stevie Wonder, and Dave Brubeck
with their innovative melodies and harmonies
yet with echoes unmistakable
coming down through the ages?
I see him now, his big arms folded,
his face bathed in a glorious sunlight,
and he sways his large tummy back and forth,
back and forth to the music.
And to his genius self he softly says,
Three centuries and here we are today.
What a joy! Toss the bouquet!

## Ruth's Gentle Plea

Here we are
on the cool grass of the common.
It's good to have you back.
A blues group has been playing,
and the harmonica is great.
Our little Johnny has been
kicking the ball with the other kids,
and dear Frank Jr., now a first grader,
was studying the sound equipment
with an intensity beyond his years.
Come lie with us.

Yesterday, before you arrived,
the boys and I were at the house
sitting near the swing in the maple tree.
They remember when they were little
and you gave them easy pushes.
They said you had made them daring
young men on the flying trapeze.

We want you to come home,
and be with us all the time.
I know you blame yourself every day.
But we could learn to deal with it,
not forgotten, of course, but past.
You are the part of us lost now.
You could be alone when you needed.
Here, come lie with us.

*With appreciation for William Kennedy*

# A Billboard Along US 301

The old professor thought it was
time to take the question seriously
as he passed the Border motel
and headed into South Carolina.
"Do you love Jesus?"
asked the big billboard on the right.
He'd seen the sign many times.

He had once been religious.
But he'd failed at churchgoing
for many decades now,
except for the frequent funerals.
Still, the billboard prodded him.
He thought the real question
the billboard was asking him was
about his relationship with Jesus.

Well, if he had one at all,
he doubted it was the Jesus
of divinity and messiah.
Or the Jesus of sins, salvation,
resurrection and everlasting life.
Nor could he imagine Jesus
as a buddy walking with him,
as wonderful as that would be.
And he couldn't warm to the Jesus
of the prayer book creeds
read so often and saying zero
about living, caring, and loving.

But there was more to consider—
things that had mattered to him.
He wondered if he would have
the courage of Jesus' Samaritan.
Would he rush to a burning car?
What about the Jesus who gave
us the Sermon on the Mount?
His favorite lapel button said,
"The meek are getting ready."
But had he lived the Beatitudes?
This Jesus had challenged him.

He also recalled well the Jesus who
kicked the bankers from the temple,
befriended Mary of Magdala,
died painfully for what he believed,
and whose closest followers,
seeking to carry on his example,
gave all their possessions to the needy.
He was surprised by his answer to
the question the billboard asked.

## High Summer

High summer made it here again,
season of yellow all around.
The sunflowers begin to bend,
the goldenrods abound.

Season of yellow all around,
day lilies bright yellow and gold,
the goldenrods abound.
The monarchs' stories to be told.

Day lilies bright yellow and gold,
swallowtail and buttercup.
The monarchs' stories to be told.
Susan's black eyes looking up.

Swallowtail and buttercup,
I marvel at what my eye now sees.
Susan's black eyes looking up,
soon yellow in the trees.

I marvel at what my eye now sees.
The sunflowers begin to bend,
soon yellow in the trees.
High summer made it here again.

## The Novelist at Bay Blues

I didn't read the paper
Didn't watch the news
Didn't wash the dog
Didn't put on shoes
Didn't call my kids
Didn't pay the dues
Didn't do my workout
Because l read my damn reviews
I read the damn reviews
Lord, I know I had to do it
But I'm sinking in the blues
Sinking in these blues

Maybe there's a better way
Not wallowing in despair
I know I'm such a slovenly cuss
The writing's where I care
Writing's where I care
The critics, they have sold me short
And for sure I need the bread
So let's pull me back together
And let's get me out of bed
More there must surely be
A new story to be shared
New stories to be shared

## So It Goes

We proceed each morning
with our everyday lives,
trailed by shadows
of what we once contrived.

Big plans, plans not so big,
brains working all the time.
They make us who we are.
Will plans and history rhyme?

Some plans made to please,
others we'd not advise.
Yet some turned out to bring
true blessings in disguise.

Your boy was rejected
at the college of your choice.
It was at the other place
that your son found his voice.

The job you badly wanted
did not materialize.
That loss was a gift
you came soon to realize.

There's the girl long forgot.
Your head was over heels.
Married now for fifty years,
that bell of true love peals!

Happiness comes in packages,
you did not place the order.
It just arrives unbeckoned
like the kiss from your daughter.

# Howl

## Greetings

What do we say on the Holiday card?
That we are well and filled with life's joys,
That we are truly, truly worried,
That we are blessed with close friends and real food,
That we are trying to cope with a ravaged democracy,
That we love to travel where nature is still strong,
That we are having trouble finding unbleached coral,
That we are thankful for good schools and medical care,
That we see such deprivation amidst extravagance,
That our expectations are defiantly high,
That we must make this year a year to realize them,
That we are young at heart and full of fight,
Yes! all That plus our great fondness and best hopes for our friends.
What a lovely bunch you are!

# A Place Beyond

Beyond all our fears, it is.
Beyond grieving and crying, it is.
Beyond even hope, it is.
What then is left beyond?

A collapse of sentiment?
What do they feel:
the black man in solitary,
the young girl buried
in the rubble of Aleppo,
the Amazon biologist
watching the forest die?

What do we feel, you and I?
Can the mere knowledge
of the world's desperation
while still in a sheltered space
take us to a place beyond?

I can only speak for myself.
I hunger to strike a blow
so shattering that enthrallment
breaks into a million shards
and falls to the feet of the world,
illusions gone, apathy impossible.

## The Strategy: A Conversation

The situation is hopeless…
and therein lies the hope.

*You are writing again!*
*But in riddles now.*

Yes.
America is in steep decline.
Failure is all around.
But that opens many doors,
something new can be born.

*That would surely be nice.*
*But is it "can" or "will"?*

Only "can."

*What will make the difference?*

You know as well as I,
vision, preparation,
struggle, sacrifice.

*Sacrifice?*

Yes. The civil rights struggle,
the fight against apartheid,
they put it all on the line.

*So, it's into the streets?*

Yes, there, everywhere
civic unreasonableness,
fearless and far-reaching.

## It's Already Tomorrow

it's already tomorrow
but you know that
we failed the moment
way back yesterday
we were young brash smart
we thought we knew
so was the fatal flaw
hubris or over-confidence
some say yes but I think
the fatal flaw was faith
that our system of political economy
had a brain big enough and feral enough
to seek its own preservation
so the system would work
at least to hold off the worst
but no nowhere near so
tomorrow is now deciding
the system is yesterday
in its pain and grief and suffering
it will banish the system
to some unheralded past
the ash heap of history

## Unnatural Order

An ugly sense of superiority
has long infected humanity.
It conveys special status,
grounds claims of privilege,
and justifies exploitation.
When it's threatened,
the fear prompts repression.

Superiority demands the inferior:
nature inferior to humans,
women inferior to men,
people of color inferior to whites.
That is the proper order of things,
or so the last of them still believe.

Now we see the old, decrepit order
crumbling everywhere we look:
rights too long denied reclaimed.
Rising protests express new joy,
anger formed of new empowerment.

Repression again seeks a foothold.
It cannot match this pregnant moment.

## New Consciousness

Decades of discourse
led by people like me
lawyers, scientists, economists
and we are stuck.

They can't do what must be done:
reach the human heart.
The deep problems are
avarice, arrogance and apathy,
dominant values badly astray.

What we need is not more analysis
but a spiritual awakening to a new consciousness.
So let's bring on the preachers and prophets!
the poets and philosophers!
the psychologists and psychiatrists!
Let's bring on the writers, musicians, actors, artists!

Call them to strike the chords of our shared humanity,
of our close kin to wild things!

## Louisiana Climate Change Blues

My house's right here on the marsh,
the water's coming up to me.
Only just a matter of time
'til I hear the slapping of the sea.

Oh Momma, oh Momma—
Momma's got to move away.
It's got way too hot in here,
she needs a cooler place to stay.

I know that I been screwed again.

I got the Louisiana climate change blues.
It's taking away my world,
it's taking my world away,
it's taking my world away.

I got to find fish for a living,
I try to find crab too.
But now they're not swimming,
not bringing fish to you.

The hurricane was such a big one,
my boat's a total wreck.
I know no one is watching out for me,
but I never did suspect.

I know that I been screwed again.
I got the Louisiana climate change blues.

# Next

a new day underway
building in the shadows
just over the horizon
piece by piece
place by place
stunning in what it asks of us
in cities not well known
in churches with half members
in councils long forgotten
in families once apart
in unions nearly crushed
in co-ops gone to seed
we see new life
rising up
up rising
many local initiatives now
coming together as new systems
systems of ownership by workers
of health care and education without division
of needs met without consumerism
of economy without growthmania
of energy without pollution
of reverence for nature's miracle
of commitment to climate's protection
of coping together with pandemics
systems of popular sovereignty
yes democracy of by and for all the people

all the people
sharing supporting caring giving loving working creating
participating debating voting demanding protesting provoking
listening learning playing worshiping trying crying trying again
tolerating respecting empathizing honoring being people
people of all races and genders and religions
bound together by good laws and good fellowship
laughter and song

## Isle of Hope

An Irish village, it's been said,
can be but a pub and a post.
Staying once in such a place
near the Connemara dreamscape,
we found two pubs side-by-side,
one serving mainly Guinness,
one serving mainly food,
no one complaining.

The bright music in the pubs there
and in other west coast towns
can move away the gloomy weather
and clear away your troubles too.
Until they sing about Annie Moore.

Annie was an Irish girl of 17
who was the first ever to walk
through to America at Ellis Island.
And so she enters our fractured hearts.
"Isle of hope, isle of tears,
isle of freedom, isle of fears."

Many thought the Irish an inferior race
when Annie disembarked in 1892.
Are we walking with her today?
Will we take her hand
and lift a light beside the Golden Door?

# Shootings

To avoid repeated interruptions,
the networks have decided
to announce the week's shootings
on Thursdays at 1 p.m.

We sprang from a wild
and reptilian thing with
long teeth and no pity.
We must deal with it.

Somewhere along the way
up our longest family tree,
an ancestor found the path
of nurture and affection.

Mother strokes the child's cheek,
the first smile appears.
A boy practices his swimming strokes,
Father holds him in the water.

The world bends with the weight
of massive contradiction.
It rights itself again—then sings,
held in the joy of music.

*Hey! Nelly Ho! Nelly*
*Listen love to me*
*I'll sing for you, play for you*
*A dulcet melody*
*Nelly Bly has a heart*
*Warm as a cup of tea*
*Bigger than a sweet potato*
*Down in Tennessee*

## Banners Yet To Be Unfurled

The snow lies lightly on the lilacs
round by the kitchen door.
The juncos peck in stone cracks
endless in their search for more.

I think that is my way too,
to keep the search going on.
What else really could I do
but find new ways to scorn?

As Camus said of Sisyphus
who toiled with his stone,
there is no fate for us
that can't be beat by scorn.

And so I scorn what passes here today
for equality and justice before the law,
for helping the poor to find a way,
for promises the troops will soon withdraw.

Most politicians are pathetic souls;
almost every sentence is a lie.
Recognition is their main goal.
To integrity they've said good-bye.

Oh purple mountain majesty!
Oh fruited plains of amber grain!
The machine crushes endlessly
everything for investment's gain.

And so we search for ways to fight.
We see the beauty of the snow,
but we know to make it right
may require our blood to flow.

We've seen the heads bandaged round,
the men and women teared by gas.
Each has earned a special crown.
They know the system will not last.

Scorn, rage, and many actions:
protests coming round the world.
Today we see but a fraction
of banners yet to be unfurled!

(This poem is from *What We Have Instead.*)

# Laugh

# Climate Negotiations

Brazil's new plans for Amazon destruction
are what prompted its abrupt decision
not to host world climate negotiations.

Now the small island nation of Jose Cuervo
has become an international hero
for bravely stepping into the breach.

Its main proffers are, first, its beach
with cabanas to watch the erosion.
Then, diving on reefs newly bleached,

the few fish now caught by explosions.
But most important for negotiators *arriva*:
unlimited quantities of blue agave tequila!

## God's Own Black Flies

God walked into the garden.
He saw that it was good.
Mostly.

He noticed that horned tomato worms
were decimating the plants and
beetles were ruining his potatoes.

Leaning down, He asked them loudly,
"Who the hell made you?"

And in that moment they found Him.
A natural poet, He cried out:

"Black flies, black flies, you're here again!
You found my forehead and my chin.
Black flies, black flies, oh, what a pest.
It's time you guys *also* took a rest."

And then the devil tempted Him—

"Black flies, I want you to go for hair
that's orange in the atmosphere.
Not a little girl's, for sure,
but a man far more immature!"

His good nature soon returning,
God remembered his Creation.
He paused, thought, and said wistfully,

"Black flies, if only I could clearly see
you as part of biodiversity!"

# Can the Poet Let the Poem Write Itself?

Hi, Poem. I'm trying
not to think of you, but
I hope you are thinking
of me. Together, you and I
are supposed to capture
a pause-worthy reality.

The best way forward,
I have heard, is for me
to be almost in a trance,
see you with a side-ways glance,
not straight on eye-to-eye,
while you, Poem, write yourself,
and I step back and let you try.

Poem, you could be a poem
about a poet and a poem who
can't quite rise to the moment.
Here's one route.
(Far from letting you go with the flow,
I seem to be showing you a place to go.)

"The poem could not get through the door.
It complained bitterly to the landlord.
She replied, 'you've got to do more!
Or instead, you could just puddle on the floor
or slide away like the watch of Salvador.'"

## As Soon as I Get Well

When I get well,
I'm going to be insufferable!
When my legs work again,
"let's scramble up that hill"
will be heard once more,
as my kids roll their eyes.
When my endurance returns,
I will challenge Cas to a fast 10K.
When I have found my balance,
I will take on Jim down the
Youghiogheny in rubber duckies,
and dare Char to join me
skreeing in the Rockies.
When my libido returns,
well, that will be interesting.
When I am at full strength again,
I'm pushing this walker to Goodwill
and organizing some touch football.
I don't think I was made to sit here
in the recliner in front of the TV
looking at Wheel of Fortune and
dying with each awful bit of news.
So get ready world!
I expect to be back any day now.

# All You Need To Know About Information Technology

As it constantly grew ahead of me,
I have climbed the mountain of IT.
But from the small peak I have reached,
I see that climb going to infinity.
So I give up here on learning more.
I'm as techy as I will ever be.

My new iPhone can do so many things
way beyond my comprehension.
I am happy to know that that is so,
but I can't give it more attention.

Facebook is enwrapped in scandal,
but it's such a money maker!
It takes your personal information
and quickly sells to any taker.

I have never written a Tweet.
Twitter will stay beyond the pale.
I have already seen too many Tweets
from senders who should be in jail.

So I step off the uphill train
and walk onto the platform.
From that point on I'll just admire
the techy things my son Jim performs.

## Half Naked and Other Moments of Zen

Early in Michaelmas term
the Dean said with a touch of wit,
"I do not care if you walk on the grass,
but you may not walk across it."
Well, that was a rule of great clarity.
So we bought some Scotch eggs and
warm bitter from the buttery,
found a nice open spot on the grass,
lay down on our backs, and tried not
to think about the afternoon class.

Part way through my lecture,
I was confronted by a heckler,
"I don't believe in global warming!"
At such points I reply about science
and trot out my most charming.
But this once I paused hardly a bit,
"Global warming doesn't care at all
whether or not you believe in it."
That felt good, and is the nicest way
I've called someone a first class twit.

I try to do what my doctor says,
and I keep good dogs at my feet.
I try too to be one who cares
and pays attention to what he eats.
But a person's got to take some chances
and dance now and then to the devil's beat.
While I've cut out the cannabis trances,
I once was stopped half naked on Main Street.

## From a Child's Garden of Sensible Verse

My Mom and Dad keep telling me
the person I must grow up to be.
They made a list of things to do.
One is to double knot my shoe.
Another is to learn to hear
which words are good
and which are swear.
My parents seem to use them all.
Damn, I swear that takes some gall!

They say the laws of nature don't allow
a bug to become a cow.
Then, they must explain to me why
I see this yellow butterfly.
They say the sky is ablaze,
but I believe it's cold up there.
They say the human mind is beautiful.
Not with all the things I hear!
Perhaps I'm young to be so jaded,
but truth and error seem so conflated.

I was wandering carefree and happy,
but now I realize that I am lost.
I hope they find me pretty snappy
or there will be big costs.
The goldfish will not be fed,
and I won't have a proper bed.
But the biggest cost will surely be
the fun they'll make of little me.
I might be alive or maybe dead.
Either, I'll have lost my local cred.

## Post-Op 2018

Suddenly awake!
Hospital's a blur.
Pain cautions: don't stir.

So I lie here medicated,
still not concentrated,
much less authenticated.

TV's turned to something dinky.
Then, two strange men in Helsinki.
The bald one says "not me."
The orange one says, "You see!"
I cry, "please, no more TV!"

Recalling now a dream of mine:
as the surgeon was removing
generous portions of my spine,
a powerful Vermont woodsman
in a wool and worn plaid shirt
and holding a sharp chainsaw,
someone I knew rather well
but could not exactly tell,
mounted my back gracefully,
knees on my shoulder blades,
and started sawing at my spine,
removing triangles perfectly
holding a smile the whole time.

The surgeon says it was a big success.
Has one ever said anything much less?

## Bad Italian

We had a dinner party on our porch.
The temp was hot enough to scorch.
I asked several if they would like
a Citronella on ice,
and they all said, "Yes,
that would be nice."

I went inside to get the Citronella
where I found the Limoncello.
*Dio mio. Dio mio.*
I was quite a dolt to so misthink,
and how should we consider now
those who wanted such a drink?

# Remember

# Getting Close

A half century ago my wife and I walked up
Jack Mountain into an unexplored meadow.
I held my little girl's hand in mine,
we carried our young sons on our backs.
It was summer, our sweatbands were
drenched, and we were exhausted. Still,

the scene ahead as we entered the meadow
startled us: everywhere white daisies
and Queen Anne's Lace, black-eyed Susans,
yellow yarrow, pink aster, purple thistle,
orange hawkweed and early goldenrod.
Our young daughter looked up at us and asked—

"Are we in Heaven?"

Just yesterday I was walking an old
logging road that runs uphill through
some green shade-dappled saplings
and opens out to a big meadow on top.
As I approached the meadow on the ridge,
all I could see ahead was the late day sun

sitting, pausing on the crest of the hill
and pouring a blinding gold over the horizon.
I just stood there in the saffron glow.
Two dark silhouettes were on the ridge top.
It took a second but then I recognized
my dogs standing there and waiting for me.

## Sunday Morning

The old man kept his balance
moving across the smooth rocks
on the far bank of the Margaree
along a wide bend in the river.

Since first light he had been
fishing the magnificent river.
The cloak of morning mist,
the feel of his favorite fly rod,
his procession down the swirling water,
the birdsong from the banks,
the salmon pools he knew so well,
it left him feeling renewed, himself.

Over the years he had come
to see the river as close to magic.
His concerns seemed to vanish
when he waded into the water.

Now he was headed for a wooden bench
someone had built long ago
where the river started to curve.
He knew that his dog Jez was lying
by the bench on the warming rocks,
as were the butter tart and hot tea.
Jez's golden color blended with the rocks,
like she was meant to be there.

He felt good about the decades he'd spent
in masonry and construction locally.
He was justified, he reckoned,
by his useful, thoughtful work,
and there had been a lot of that.
But he had made time for fishing,
and he was very glad he had.

It was Sunday and his wife, half jokingly,
had said he should be going to church.
He thought of that as he sat on the bench.
He could still make church if he left now.
But he felt he needed more time with the river.
"You don't have much conflict about it, Jez.
I can see that," he murmured.

He looked up through the tree canopy
to the sky brightening up,
and he thought, not for the first time,
that he was in church already.
He gave a small piece of the tart to Jez,
took a sip of the steaming tea, and
focused down the river where the
sunlight now danced on the water.

## Aunt Ginny's Story

The old maple we planted by the house
a long, long time ago
took a heavy beating last summer.
The children who climbed it
and played in its limbs each summer
did not make it here.

Not then. Not again.

Could it feel the aching sadness
that spread every day from the house into the yard?
Did it miss the grab of little hands,
the press of sneakers, the scraped knees,
the rocking of the swing?
Who can say?  I can only report that

its leaves did not turn red last fall.

They simply went to brown, crumpled, and fell.
We talked about how it might not recover.
We talked about cutting it for firewood,
something useful, a good ending.
We talked about a lot of things.

I doubt that I'd be telling this story
if the maple hadn't leafed out in the spring.
Not gloriously, but there it was:
life returning, awaiting.
Its leaves were smaller,
more delicate, but it was back.
We could see that.

# From NYC to Vermont

I saw him sliding seamlessly
through the Broadway crowd.
What to make of him?
He seemed more proud than bowed.
Worlds are made of words,
and he's been a great maker.
But he's led a life of bad mistakes.
Do we stick to what he put on paper?

I imagine him in Vermont
without the screaming people
and their jangling jarring stories
without the neurotic density
to fuel his words' intensity.
Could he write among the trees?

Summer brings blue-winged teal
to the pond down by our house.
The small ducks drift behind ash branches
dabbling around, in and out.
In winter, the ravens will be croaking
among themselves near my window
fastened tightly against the cold.
Life here he could not really know.

## Thin Doors

Thin doors in our lives,
mere gossamer things
between present and past,
remembering and forgetting,
loving and despising,
living and dying.
We walk or stumble
willy-nilly through them.

———◎

The Edisto River rises in the sand hills of central South
Carolina. Like a glistening black snake it glides through
the Carolina Lowcountry. Its dark tannin-stained waters
spread out over the banks forming swamps of tall cypress,
tupelo, and sweet gum draped with Spanish moss,
an environment welcoming to its sunfish, heron, and
occasional alligators. On its way through the hardwood
bottomlands and on down to the tidal marshes, the
Edisto passes through the small agricultural community
of Orangeburg. I grew up there in the 1940s and 1950s,
our house about a mile from a swimming area the town
had established down from a high bluff. On the several
terraces from the bluff's top down to the river, the girls
spread blankets on the grass and worked on their (one-
piece) tans. Near the riverbank, benches ran between large
cypress trees where mothers sat watching their children
play in the shallow water. A pavilion on the top of the
bluff served RC Colas and hot dogs. There were pinball
machines there. The juke box played "Sixty Minute
Man," a song to fuel a boy's fantasy if there ever was one.

When I was a preschooler, my buddies and I would jump off a platform that stuck out over the river and doggy paddle back to the platform ladder. One day I got a good running start and jumped out too far, into the strength of the river's current. It carried me away fast, and soon I was underwater staring wide-eyed at the rays of sun coming through the tea-colored water and completely unable to surface or gain control. I remember thinking that I was going to drown. Back on the benches, my mother scanned the platform area, and, not finding me, she and her friend panicked and sprang for the river, Mom to the platform, her friend to the deep water where the children's swimming area ended. I remember being wrapped up into the arms of two strong women and carried out of the water and laid on my stomach on the bank, my cheek on the warm sand.

As the Edisto becomes tidal and enters the Atlantic, it flows by Seabrook Island. This coastal barrier island near Charleston, once full with the delight of maritime forests, Seabrook had been given to the sturdy Episcopal Diocese of South Carolina with the requirement that its rare natural beauty remain unspoiled. A small Episcopal summer camp for young people was the only thing on it. I went there as a camper for many summers, and I loved the place. I got to know a group of young ministers, and discussing theology with them was the most intellectually exciting thing I did as a boy. Then I went off to college. I stopped going to church, lost interest in organized religion, and realized one day I had become something akin to an atheist. The sunsets at the camp looking back up the Edisto, the loggerheads coming ashore to lay their eggs, the pluff mud up to your knees in the saltmarsh, the fiddler crabs scurrying about—all will be always with me. If I had been raised a pantheist, I might still be one. Years later, the Diocese would sell Seabrook to developers. As Faulkner wrote, the very act of selling the land should have forfeited the seller's claim to it.

My final stay at the camp was shortly after graduating from Orangeburg High in 1960. We were excited to have our bishop, Thomas Carruthers, join us in camp for a short spell. The bishop seemed a giant in every way—size, presence, booming voice—and was enjoying himself being with young people. On a hot Sunday afternoon we walked with him down to the mouth of the Edisto and around the point onto Seabrook's pristine front beach and had a cookout there. Afterwards, staff in hand, he led us back to the camp's cabins. The bishop said he was tired and went to his room in the counselors' cabin, and I joined a small group of young ministers on the cabin's porch. They were talking and I was listening. Then we heard a loud thud from inside the cabin. We all rushed to the bishop's room. Through the thin door we could hear the bishop snoring. When we tried to open the door, something held it shut. One minister said the bishop had not liked his door banging in the wind, so he must have blocked it shut with a suitcase. Another added that he had been complaining about being tired and must have gone quickly to sleep. We moved quietly back to the porch and resumed conversation. Later that night, back in my cabin, I would learn that the bishop, age 60, had died that evening of a cerebral hemorrhage. He had fallen against his door.

Immediately before reaching Seabrook Island, the Edisto passes by the settlement known as Rockville, a small gathering of very old homes and large live oak trees. It is a beautiful spot from a long-lost era and is best known still for its sailing. I have a friend who sailed his Moth in all the coastal regattas, and one summer during my high school years, he signed me on as his crew. Moths have no crew, tiny one-person boats that they are, but it got me into all the parties, including the famous dance at Rockville held after the race every August since 1890.

The Rockville clubhouse is a one-story clapboard structure in the Lowcountry style, with a large open floor for dancing. Its huge windows and porch on multiple sides make the whole thing veranda-like when opened up. As it was the evening of the dance. The band was pumping away that late 1950s night; the dance floor was crowded, mostly with young people; it was hot; and the alcohol was freely flowing. As I walked outside to cool off, I noticed couples headed for the grass and backseats of the parked cars. Feeling especially lonely after missing out on what was very close to a drunken orgy, I sat on a porch bench, next to two perspiring but well-dressed matrons. Despite the loud music, I could not help but overhear their conversation. The lady next to me said in a charming Charleston accent, "This event has gone terribly downhill." "Yes," the other agreed, "What a shame that the young men are dancing without their jackets."

## Memory's Gate

My dear,
I am trying hard to recall
where my memory went AWOL.
What is it that I forgot?
Does it still matter a lot?

It seems we'll just have to wait
'til time unlocks memory's gate.

# Reboot

I wish I could plug me in
and get me fully charged.
There is memory I need to keep,
and messages I need to send.

Old models need special care.
The interface still works,
but user-friendly means
something rather different—

a slower response time
and more time sleeping
are not the all of it.
Getting logged in
is a special problem.

The faces our cameras see
and zoom around the world
are not the old familiar ones,
but new ones weak-eyed and worn
from searching, staring, scrolling.

I fear the dreaded crash,
a loss of precious information,
perhaps unrecoverable for all time.
One crash too many and
there is nothing left to upload.

## The Last Monarch

The season of beautiful endings,
life giving up another round.
At first it seemed heart rending.
The fields turned a rusty brown.

Life giving up another round,
the monarch drifted to the grass.
The fields turned a rusty brown.
Fall has now yes come to pass.

The monarch drifted to the grass,
the maples glowed bright red.
Fall has now yes come to pass,
nature putting herself to bed.

The maples glowed bright red.
Dying away precedes new birth,
nature putting herself to bed.
My footprint too upon this earth.

Dying away precedes new birth,
at first it seemed heart rending.
My footprint too upon this earth.
This season of beautiful endings.

## The Prince of Tides

Wishing to pay our respects
to a writer not long departed,
we stood on a Carolina sea island
not far from where he began,
his friend Reverend Mike and I,
there on an early spring day.
Mike had been there before,
but to me a joyous surprise.

> *I was born and raised on a Carolina sea island and
> I carried the sunshine of the low country, inked in
> dark gold, on my back and shoulders....My sister and
> I... were born to a house of complication, drama, and
> pain. We were typical southerners. In every southerner,
> beneath the veneer of cliché lies a much deeper
> motherload of cliché.*

I shuffled my feet and sand
drifted across his simple grave.
We were in the middle of an acre
cleared from maritime forest—
an isolated black cemetery,
burial mounds scattered around.
How had the entertainer of millions
come to this unknown spot to rest?

> *I ... take you to the marsh on a spring day, flush the great
> blue heron from its silent occupation. Scatter marsh hens
> as we sink to our knees in mud, open you an oyster with
> a pocketknife and feed it to you from the shell and say,
> "There. That taste. That's the taste of my childhood." I
> would say, "Breathe deeply," and you would breathe and
> remember that smell for the rest of your life.*

The wind rustled the magnolia leaves.
It had crossed the incoming tide,
alive with spot tail bass and shrimp,
drifted over sun-filled marshes of spartina,
picked up the dank smell of pluff mud
and the chatter of cedar waxwings.
In such a familiar and peaceful place,
he must have felt his demons released.

> *Anytime I would come into the house with a string of fish...*
> *my mother could not have been more upset if I had*
> *brought roadkill newly scraped off the highway...*
> *Each fresh tide brought shoals of white shrimp boiling*
> *into the creeks a hundred yards from the house where*
> *my mother heated up their frozen cousins.*

I too was smitten by that quiet place—
Mike said there was much more to say.
We were surrounded there by landmarks
in the history of people once shackled,
including the site of the famous Penn School
for those newly freed from enslavement.
His books tell stories of whites;
his death celebrates the stories of blacks.

> *Teaching remains a heroic act to me, and teachers live a*
> *necessary and all-important life. ...Long ago I was one of*
> *them. I still regret I was forced to leave them. My entire*
> *body of work is because of men and women like them....*
> *Though I've never met a teacher who was not happy in*
> *retirement, I rarely meet one who thinks that their teaching*
> *was not a grand way to spend a human life.*

I see that I am not the first to visit
this remote and secluded gravesite.
The once bare mound of sandy loam
that defines his last place
is covered now with mementoes,
gifts from guests like me—
an oyster shell, a fishhook, a shrimp boat,
a little b-ball, other notes of grace.

> *On the top shelf, I spotted Savannah's second book*
> *of poetry,* The Prince of Tides. *I opened it to the*
> *dedication page and almost cried when I read the words:*
>> *Man wonders but God decides*
>> *When to kill The Prince of Tides*

*(the excerpts in italics here are from Pat Conroy's writings)*

# Coronavirus, Near Charleston, March 2020

Big beachfront houses, solid,
cementitious, dug into the earth,
await the next big wind and water.

But now empty. Even the rich
cannot get onto this sea island.
Beachgoers turned quickly away.

Two old renters of an old house
shuffle down the vacant strand
alone with the surf and their dogs.

Black Skimmers, Sanderlings, Laughing Gulls—
they're still here and tempt the mind to
imagine a natural world safe from people.

But I am thinking now mainly of people,
and I am beginning to cry,
struggling with what is going on.

The great world wails,
the suffering is just starting.
What must we learn? What must we do?

Houses thought to be impregnable against climate,
a country too great to be brought low by a virus—
two artifacts of arrogance.

So many vacant spaces. Still,
our worlds are full with memories.
We will remember each other.

*With Appreciation*

I owe some big debts. I have been coached and critiqued by some of the best poets and teachers around—Ina Anderson, Richard Garcia, Sydney Lea, Catherine McCullough and Carol Potter among them. I thank them especially for their kind encouragement and good advice. Most of all I am grateful and beyond to Cece Speth, a loyal and insightful partner at every point.

*Gus Speth*
*Strafford, Vermont*
*early spring 2020*